Given to me at
Turney United
Methodist Church Tea   10/8/17

To:

_____

From:

_____

∽

Requests for information should be addressed to:
Inspirio, The gift group of Zondervan
Grand Rapids, Michigan 49530
http://www.inspiriogifts.com

Compilation and Prayers: Lisa Eary
Project Manager: Tom Dean
Design Manager: Amy Wenger
Design: Sherri L. Hoffman

Printed in the United States of America
04 /DC/ 4 3 2 1

PRAYING
the
NAMES
of
GOD

Journal

ANN
SPANGLER

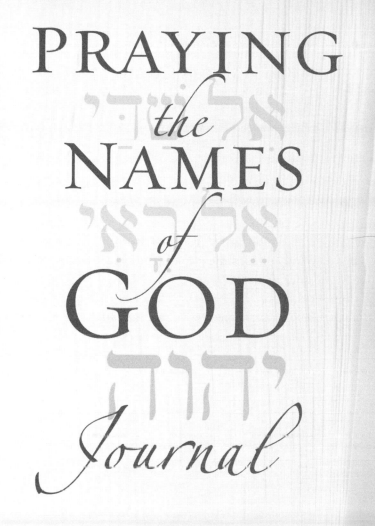

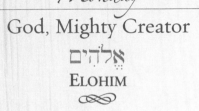

Monday
God, Mighty Creator

אֱלֹהִים

Elohim

Elohim (e-lo-HEEM) is the Hebrew word for God that appears in the very first sentence of the Bible. When we pray to *Elohim*, we remember that he is the one who began it all, creating the heavens and the earth and separating light from darkness, water from dry land, night from day. This ancient name for God contains the idea of God's creative power as well as his authority and sovereignty.

In the beginning Elohim created the heavens and the earth. —GENESIS 1:1

God, Mighty Creator
ELOHIM
∞

Understanding the Name

Read Genesis 1:1–24.

Genesis is a word that can mean "birth," "history of origin," or "genealogy." What can you observe about who God is from this passage about beginnings?

_____

_____

_____

_____

_____

_____

God seems delighted by what he has made, proclaiming it "good" and even "very good." How does God's assessment of creation shape your own attitude toward the world? Toward yourself?

_____

_____

_____

_____

_____

_____

_____

_____

_____

Tuesday
God, Mighty Creator
ELOHIM

Praying the Name

Elohim, you looked at all you created and said it was very good. From the Himalayas to DNA, everything you have made is wonderful and orderly and good.

(GENESIS 1:31)

Wednesday
God, Mighty Creator
ELOHIM

Praying the Name

Elohim, you created me, and you promise in your Word that you will be with me and watch over me wherever I go. You are the God who keeps his promises.

(GENESIS 28:15)

Thursday
God, Mighty Creator
ELOHIM

Praying the Name

Elohim, you are the one who laid the foundations of the earth, and the heavens above are the work of your hands. Great as they are, you are greater still. Someday you will sweep them all away. But you will remain—*forever*.

(PSALM 102:25–26)

Friday

God, Mighty Creator

ELOHIM

∞

Promises Associated with *Elohim*

Do you not know?
  Have you not heard?
The LORD is the everlasting God,
  the Creator of the ends of the earth.
He will not grow tired or weary,
  and his understanding no one can fathom.
He gives strength to the weary
  and increases the power of the weak.

—ISAIAH 40:28–29

So do not fear, for I am with you;
  do not be dismayed, for I am your God.
I will strengthen you and help you;
  I will uphold you with my righteous right hand.

—ISAIAH 41:10

I will not leave you until I have done what I have promised you.

—GENESIS 28:15

Monday

The God Who Sees Me

אֵל רָאִי

EL ROI

∞

Hagar, Sarah's Egyptian slave, encountered God in the desert and addressed him as *El Roi* (EL ro-EE), "the God who sees me." In the midst of her difficulties, Hagar learned that *El Roi* was watching over her and that he had a plan to bless her and her son. Hagar's God is the one who numbers the hairs on our heads and who knows our circumstances, past, present, and future. When you pray to *El Roi,* you are praying to the one who knows everything about you.

Hagar gave this name to the LORD who spoke to her: "You are El Roi," for she said, "I have now seen the One who sees me." —GENESIS 16:13

The God Who Sees Me
El Roi
❀

Understanding the Name

Read Genesis 16:1–16.

What images immediately come to mind when you hear the name *El Roi,* "the God who sees me"?

_____

_____

_____

_____

_____

_____

_____

How have you experienced God's watchful care?

_____

_____

_____

_____

_____

_____

_____

_____

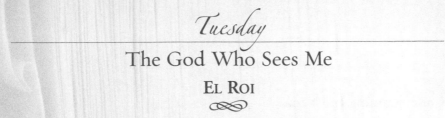

Tuesday

The God Who Sees Me

EL ROI

Praying the Name

El Roi, you know where I have come from and where I am going. You know the things that frighten me. You guide me in the midst of my troubles. You comfort me with your promises and your love.

(GENESIS 16:8–10)

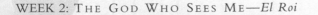

Wednesday
The God Who Sees Me
El Roi
∞

Praying the Name

El Roi, you see my tears and hear my prayers. Open my eyes and show me all the ways you answer my prayers and meet my needs, even when I don't ask.

(GENESIS 21:17–19)

Thursday

The God Who Sees Me
El Roi
∞

Praying the Name

El Roi, your eyes are on those who honor you and who put their hope in your unfailing love. Help me to remember this and trust you to deliver me.

(PSALM 33:18–19)

Friday

The God Who Sees Me
EL ROI

Promises Associated with *El Roi*

For the eyes of the LORD range throughout the earth to strengthen those whose hearts are fully committed to him. —2 CHRONICLES 16:9

> The LORD watches over you—
>   the LORD is your shade at your right hand;
> the sun will not harm you by day,
>   nor the moon by night.
> The LORD will keep you from all harm—
>   he will watch over your life;
> the LORD will watch over your coming and going
>   both now and forevermore.
>   —PSALM 121:5–8

> The eyes of the LORD are everywhere,
>   keeping watch on the wicked and the good.
>   —PROVERBS 15:3

God Almighty

אֵל שַׁדַּי

EL SHADDAY

The Hebrew *El Shadday* (EL sha-DAI), often translated "God Almighty," may literally be translated "God, the Mountain One." *El Shadday* reveals God not only as the one who creates and maintains the universe, but also as the one who initiates and maintains a covenant with his people. God revealed himself as *El Shadday*, God Almighty, to Abram and told him of the everlasting covenant he was establishing with him and with his descendants. When we pray to *El Shadday*, we invoke the name of the one for whom nothing is impossible.

When Abram was ninety-nine years old, the LORD appeared to him and said, "I am El Shadday; walk before me and be blameless. I will confirm my covenant between me and you and will greatly increase your numbers."

—GENESIS 17:1–2

God Almighty
EL SHADDAY
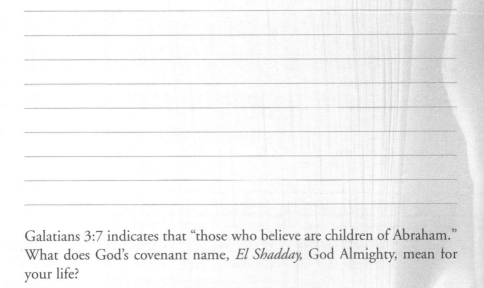

Understanding the Name

Read Genesis 17:1–8.

What was Abraham's response to the promise and the revelation of God's name? How do you think you would have responded if God had revealed himself to you as he did to Abraham?

_____

_____

_____

_____

_____

_____

_____

Galatians 3:7 indicates that "those who believe are children of Abraham." What does God's covenant name, *El Shadday*, God Almighty, mean for your life?

_____

_____

_____

_____

_____

_____

_____

Tuesday
God Almighty
EL SHADDAY

Praying the Name

You are *El Shadday*. Yet you have made a covenant with me, to save me and bind me to you through Jesus—*forever*. I fall facedown before you. Help me to bring honor to your name.

(GENESIS 17:1–3)

Wednesday
God Almighty
EL SHADDAY

Praying the Name

El Shadday, you are my refuge and my fortress, my God, in whom I trust.
I place myself under your protection so that I may always be at rest in your
presence, Almighty God, no matter what happens in my life.

(PSALM 91:1–2)

Thursday
God Almighty
El Shadday

Praying the Name

El Shadday, you have shown your power by blessing my life over and over.
You give me victory over sin and other troubles of this world. But most
of all, you bless me with the power of your presence in my life.

(GENESIS 49:24–25)

Friday

God Almighty

EL SHADDAY

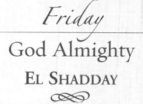

Promises Associated with *El Shadday*

The name of the Lord is a strong tower;
the righteous run to it and are safe.

—PROVERBS 18:10

I will make you into a great nation
and I will bless you;
I will make your name great,
and you will be a blessing.
I will bless those who bless you,
and whoever curses you I will curse;
and all peoples on earth
will be blessed through you.

—GENESIS 12:2-3

I will surely bless you and make your descendants as numerous as the stars in
the sky and as the sand on the seashore. —GENESIS 22:17

The Everlasting God or The Eternal God

אֵל עוֹלָם

EL OLAM

∞

Olam is a Hebrew word that occurs more than four hundred times in the Old Testament. It is translated as "eternal," "everlasting," "forever," "lasting," "ever," or "ancient." It refers to the fullness of the experience of time or space. *El Olam* (EL o-LAM) is the Hebrew name for the God who has no beginning and no end, the God for whom a day is as a thousand years and a thousand years are as a day. When you pray to the Everlasting God, you are praying to the God whose love endures forever.

After the treaty had been made at Beersheba, Abimelech and Phicol the commander of his forces returned to the land of the Philistines. Abraham planted a tamarisk tree in Beersheba, and there he called upon the name of the LORD, El Olam. —GENESIS 21:32–33

The Everlasting God or The Eternal God
El Olam
❦

Understanding the Name

Read Genesis 21:22–34.

Beersheba means "well of the oath." Why do you think Abraham planted a tamarisk (a relatively long-living tree) after the two men swore an oath about Abraham's well?

_____

_____

_____

_____

_____

_____

_____

_____

What might the name *El Olam* imply about the nature of God's promises?

_____

_____

_____

_____

_____

_____

_____

_____

_____

_____

Tuesday

The Everlasting God or The Eternal God
EL OLAM
∞

Praying the Name

El Olam, I can't imagine what it would be like to live a thousand years, yet to you a thousand years are like one day that has just gone by. Help me to understand the concept of *everlasting.* Teach me how to live the life you have given me—where every day matters for eternity.

(PSALM 90:4, 12)

Wednesday
The Everlasting God or The Eternal God
El Olam

Praying the Name

El Olam, you always have been, always are, and always will be. You never grow tired or weary, and you understand the entire universe and everything in it. When I am weak and weary, you give your everlasting strength to me—and you always will.

(ISAIAH 40:28–29)

Thursday

The Everlasting God or The Eternal God
EL OLAM

Praying the Name

El Olam, eternal life is knowing you. And you have made it possible for me to know you through your Son, Jesus Christ, whom you sent into the world. *El Olam,* the only true God, what greater gift is there than knowing you forever?

(JOHN 17:3)

Friday

The Everlasting God or The Eternal God

EL OLAM

∞

Promises Associated with *El Olam*

> But the plans of the LORD stand firm forever,
> the purposes of his heart through all generations.
> —PSALM 33:11

> For my Father's will is that everyone who looks to the Son and believes in him
> shall have eternal life, and I will raise him up at the last day.
> —JOHN 6:40

> Enter his gates with thanksgiving
> and his courts with praise;
> give thanks to him and praise his name.
> For the LORD is good and his love endures forever.
> —PSALM 100:4-5

Monday

The LORD Will Provide

יהוה יִרְאֶה

YAHWEH YIREH

The Hebrew word *raah* (RA-ah, from which *yireh* is derived) means "to see." Since God sees the future as well as the past and the present, he is able to anticipate and provide for what is needed. *Yahweh Yireh* (yah-WEH yir-EH) provided the one sacrifice that would make our peace with him. When you pray to *Yahweh Yireh,* you are praying to the God who sees the situation beforehand and is able to provide for your needs.

Abraham looked up and there in a thicket he saw a ram caught by its horns. He went over and took the ram and sacrificed it as a burnt offering instead of his son. So Abraham called that place Yahweh Yireh. And to this day it is said, "On the mountain of the LORD it will be provided." —GENESIS 22:13–14

The LORD Will Provide

YAHWEH YIREH

∞

Understanding the Name

Read Genesis 22:1–14.

Imagine that you are Abraham, making the three-day trip toward Moriah to sacrifice your son. What is in your heart?

_____

_____

_____

_____

_____

_____

_____

_____

In what ways has God provided for you?

_____

_____

_____

_____

_____

_____

_____

_____

_____

_____

Tuesday
The LORD Will Provide
YAHWEH YIREH

Praying the Name

Yahweh Yireh, just as you provided a ram for Abraham to sacrifice instead of his own son, you have provided a sacrifice for my sins. On that same mountain, you gave your Son, whose death restores me to life.

(GENESIS 22:13–14)

Wednesday
The LORD Will Provide
YAHWEH YIREH

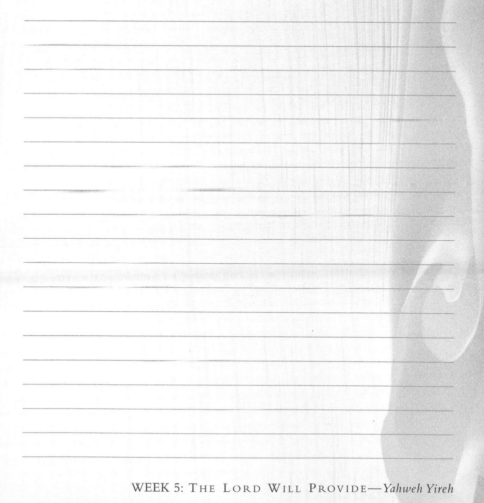

Praying the Name

Yahweh Yireh, you tested Abraham to see if he was willing to give you the most precious thing in his life. Help me to love you so much that I am willing to give up everything for you, the one who provides everything for me.

(GENESIS 22:9–12)

Thursday
The LORD Will Provide
YAHWEH YIREH

∞

Praying the Name

Yahweh Yireh, you promised to bless Abraham because of his obedience, and through his obedience, I am blessed. Please continue to provide for me and use my obedience to bless others.

(GENESIS 22:16–18)

Friday

The LORD Will Provide

YAHWEH YIREH

∞

Promises Associated with *Yahweh Yireh*

For in the land the LORD your God is giving you to possess as your inheritance, he will richly bless you, if only you fully obey the LORD your God and are careful to follow all these commands I am giving you today.

—DEUTERONOMY 15:4–6

For the LORD has chosen Zion,
  he has desired it for his dwelling:
"This is my resting place for ever and ever;
  here I will sit enthroned, for I have desired it—
I will bless her with abundant provisions;
  her poor will I satisfy with food."

—PSALM 132:13–15

So, if you think you are standing firm, be careful that you don't fall! No temptation has seized you except what is common to man. And God is faithful; he will not let you be tempted beyond what you can bear. But when you are tempted, he will also provide a way out so that you can stand up under it.

—1 CORINTHIANS 10:12–13

Monday

LORD

יהוה

YAHWEH

∞

The name *Yahweh* (yah-WEH) occurs more than 6,800 times in the Old Testament. *Yahweh* is the name that is most closely linked to God's redeeming acts in the history of his chosen people. *Yahweh* is not remote or aloof, but always near, intervening in history on behalf of his people. The name *Yahweh* evokes images of God's saving power in the lives of his people. We know God because of what he has done. When you pray to *Yahweh*, remember that he is the same God who draws near to save you from the tyranny of sin, just as he saved his people from slavery in Egypt.

God said to Moses, "I AM WHO I AM. This is what you are to say to the Israelites: 'I AM has sent me to you.'"

God also said to Moses, "Say to the Israelites, 'Yahweh, the God of your fathers—the God of Abraham, the God of Isaac and the God of Jacob—has sent me to you.' This is my name forever, the name by which I am to be remembered from generation to generation." —EXODUS 3:14–15

LORD
YAHWEH
∞

Understanding the Name

Read Exodus 3:1–20.

What does this passage reveal about what was in the heart of God with regard to his people?

_____

_____

_____

_____

_____

_____

_____

_____

_____

Why do you think Moses asked God to reveal his name?

_____

_____

_____

_____

_____

_____

_____

_____

_____

_____

Tuesday
LORD
YAHWEH

Praying the Name

Yahweh, just as you brought Israel out of slavery in Egypt with a mighty hand and made them your people, so you have brought me out of slavery to sin and made me your child. Help me to remember this and to worship you for your saving power.

(EXODUS 20:2–3)

Wednesday
LORD
YAHWEH

Praying the Name

I praise you, *Yahweh,* with all my soul, for you have forgiven my sins and healed me; you have brought me out of the pit and shown me your love and compassion. You, *Yahweh*, satisfy my desires with good things. You are my forgiving, healing, redeeming, compassionate, gracious and loving God.

(PSALM 103:2–5)

Thursday

LORD

YAHWEH

Praying the Name

Yahweh, Jesus told us the truth. The same "I AM" whom Abraham knew, came to this earth to save us. Although the world rejected Jesus, you enable me to believe that he is "I AM"—*Yahweh*.

(JOHN 8:54–59)

_____

_____

_____

_____

_____

_____

_____

_____

_____

_____

_____

_____

_____

_____

_____

_____

_____

_____

_____

_____

Friday

LORD

YAHWEH

∞

Promises Associated with *Yahweh*

> The LORD *[Yahweh]* will be your confidence
> and will keep your foot from being snared.
> —PROVERBS 3:26

> The name of the LORD *[Yahweh]* is a strong tower;
> the righteous run to it and are safe.
> —PROVERBS 18: 10

The LORD [Yahweh] will establish you as his holy people, as he promised you on oath, if you keep the commands of the LORD [Yahweh] your God and walk in his ways.... The LORD [Yahweh] will open the heavens, the storehouse of his bounty, to send rain on your land in season and to bless all the work of your hands. —DEUTERONOMY 28:9, 12

_____

_____

_____

_____

_____

_____

_____

_____

_____

_____

_____

Monday

Lord, Master

אֲדֹנָי

ADONAY

❧

Adon is a Hebrew word that means "lord" in the sense of an owner, master, or superior. It is frequently used as a term of respect and always refers to people. *Adonay* (a-do-NAI) is the plural form of *adon* and always refers to God as Lord or Master. *Adonay* is a name that implies relationship: God is Lord, and we are his servants. As you pray to *Adonay*, tell him you want to surrender every aspect of your life to him. In fact, it is in knowing him as your Lord that you will discover a true sense of purpose. The New Testament depicts Jesus as both Lord and Servant. In this latter role he exemplifies what our relationship to *Adonay* is to be.

> *You are my Adonay;*
> *apart from you I have no good thing.*
> —PSALM 16:2

Lord, Master
ADONAY
∞

Understanding the Name

Read Exodus 4:1–15.

How is the lordship of God displayed in this passage?

_____

_____

_____

_____

_____

_____

_____

_____

Notice that Moses expressed reluctance about doing God's will at the same time he was addressing him as "Lord." Have you ever done the same thing?

_____

_____

_____

_____

_____

_____

_____

_____

_____

Tuesday
Lord, Master
ADONAY

Praying the Name

Adonay, it is my one desire to bring you glory, to serve and love you. May you increase, and I decrease. Teach me what it means to have you as my Lord.

(LUKE 17:10)

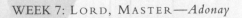

Wednesday
Lord, Master
ADONAY

Praying the Name

You are my *Adonay*. I choose to be your servant, your slave, because apart from you, I have no good thing—no joy, no peace, no protection. But with you I have everything—true purpose, power, and love.

(PSALM 16:2)

Thursday

Lord, Master

ADONAY

Praying the Name

Because you are my *Adonay*, I don't need to be afraid of my enemies. Help me to remember that your awesome power is greater than any enemy, human or spiritual. As your servant, I ask for your power to fight for my family and for you.

(NEHEMIAH 4:14)

Friday

Lord, Master

ADONAY

∞

Promises Associated with *Adonay*

The Sovereign LORD is my strength.

— HABAKKUK 3:19

Therefore, this is what the Sovereign LORD says:

> *"My servants will eat,*
>   *but you will go hungry;*
> *my servants will drink,*
>   *but you will go thirsty;*
> *my servants will rejoice,*
>   *but you will be put to shame.*
> *My servants will sing*
>   *out of the joy of their hearts,*
> *but you will cry out*
>   *from anguish of heart*
>   *and wail in brokenness of spirit."*

— ISAIAH 65:13-14

> *But you, O Lord, are a compassionate and gracious God,*
>   *slow to anger, abounding in love and faithfulness.*

— PSALM 86:15

_____

_____

_____

_____

_____

_____

_____

_____

Monday

The LORD Who Heals

יהוה רֹפֵא

YAHWEH ROPHE

∞

The Hebrew word *rophe* means to "heal," "cure," "restore," or "make whole." Although it often refers to physical healing, this word usually has a larger meaning as well, involving the entire person. Rather than merely healing the body, *Yahweh Rophe* (yah-WEH ro-FEH) heals the mind and soul. As you pray to *Yahweh Rophe*, ask him to search your heart. Take time to let him show you what it contains. If he uncovers any sin, ask his forgiveness and then pray for healing.

[The LORD] said [to Israel], "If you diligently heed the voice of the LORD your God and do what is right in His sight, give ear to His commandments and keep all His statutes, I will put none of the diseases on you which I have brought on the Egyptians. For I AM the Lord who heals you. —EXODUS 15:26, NKJV

The LORD Who Heals
YAHWEH ROPHE

Understanding the Name

Read Exodus 15:19–27.

God tested the Israelites, uncovering what was in their hearts. Describe ways in which you have experienced God's testing of you. How did you respond?

_____

_____

_____

_____

_____

_____

_____

_____

What does this passage say about God's control over sickness and health?

_____

_____

_____

_____

_____

_____

_____

_____

Tuesday
The LORD Who Heals
YAHWEH ROPHE

Praying the Name

Yahweh Rophe, you are the God who heals both body and soul. Please help me to see where my sin may be causing me to be sick. Bring me to repentance and heal me, I pray.

(EXODUS 15:26)

Wednesday
The LORD Who Heals
YAHWEH ROPHE

Praying the Name

Yahweh Rophe, you took my illnesses upon yourself. You were crucified for my sins, wounded so that I could be healed. Help me not to take my life for granted, but to realize the price you have paid.

(ISAIAH 53:4–5)

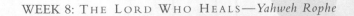

Thursday

The LORD Who Heals

YAHWEH ROPHE

Praying the Name

Yahweh Rophe, you healed me so that your work could be displayed in my life for others to see. Please help me to recognize your healing work. Help me to see how you have washed me and made me clean—for your glory.
(JOHN 9:1–7)

Friday

The LORD Who Heals

YAHWEH ROPHE

∽

Promises Associated with *Yahweh Rophe*

This is what the LORD, the God of your father David, says: I have heard your prayer and seen your tears; I will heal you.   —2 KINGS 20:5

> Praise the LORD, O my soul;
>   all my inmost being, praise his holy name.
> Praise the LORD, O my Soul,
>   and forget not all his benefits—
> who forgives all your sins
>   and heals all your diseases,
> who redeems your life from the pit
>   and crowns you with love and compassion,
> who satisfies your desires with good things
>   so that your youth is renewed like the eagle's.
>   —PSALM 103:1–5

Jesus said to Jairus, "Don't be afraid; just believe, and she will be healed."
                                    —LUKE 8:50

Is any one of you sick? He should call the elders of the church to pray over him and anoint him with oil in the name of the Lord. And the prayer offered in faith will make the sick person well; the Lord will raise him up.   JAMES 5:14–15

The LORD My Banner

יהוה נִסִּי

YAHWEH NISSI

A banner carried at the head of an army or planted on a high hill served as a rallying point for troops before battle or as an announcement of a victory already won. Because they embodied the ideals and aspirations of whoever carried them, banners aroused devotion to a nation, a cause, or a leader. When Moses held up the staff of God in the battle with the Amalekites, he was holding it like a banner, appealing to God's power. By building an altar and naming it *Yahweh Nissi* (yah-WEH nis-SEE), "The LORD is my Banner," he created a memorial of God's protection and power during the Israelites' first battle after leaving Egypt. When you pray to *Yahweh Nissi*, you are praying to the God who is powerful enough to overcome any foe.

Moses built an altar and called it Yahweh Nissi. He said, "For hands were lifted up to the throne of the LORD. The LORD will be at war against the Amalekites from generation to generation." —EXODUS 17:15–16

The LORD My Banner
YAHWEH NISSI

Understanding the Name

Read Exodus 17:8–16.

The Amalekites were fierce enemies of the Israelites. What or who are some of the enemies you face, and how have you dealt with them?

_____

_____

_____

_____

_____

_____

_____

What difference would it make if you could say, like Moses, "The LORD is my Banner"?

_____

_____

_____

_____

_____

_____

_____

_____

_____

_____

_____

Tuesday

The LORD My Banner

YAHWEH NISSI

Praying the Name

Yahweh Nissi, like Moses, I lift up my hands to your throne and ask for your help to overcome my enemies—both human and spiritual. Be my banner. Show me your presence. And help me remember that the battle is already won.

(EXODUS 17:15–16)

Wednesday
The LORD My Banner
YAHWEH NISSI

Praying the Name

Yahweh Nissi, Moses lifted up a bronze snake like a banner in the desert, and all who looked at it were healed. You raised Jesus up like a banner as well. Help me to stay focused on him so that I may have life to the full.

(JOHN 3:14–15)

Thursday
The LORD My Banner
YAHWEH NISSI

Praying the Name

Yahweh Nissi, please be a banner to those in my life who don't know you. Help them to see your banner and rally to it. Use me, too, as your banner to guide them to the truth of your love.

(ISAIAH 49:22)

Friday

The LORD My Banner

YAHWEH NISSI

∞

Promises Associated with *Yahweh Nissi*

But for those who fear you, you have raised a banner
to be unfurled against the bow.

—PSALM 60:4

You are my King and my God,
who decrees victories for Jacob.
Through you we push back our enemies;
through your name we trample our foes....
In God we make our boast all day long,
and we will praise your name forever.

—PSALM 44:4-5, 8

Monday

Consuming Fire; Jealous God

אֵשׁ אֹכְלָה, אֵל קַנָּא
ESH OKLAH, EL KANNA

❦

God sometimes manifested himself through images of fire—as a blazing torch, in the burning bush, or as a pillar of fire. Most often when Scripture pictures God as a consuming fire (*Esh Oklah*; AISH o-KLAH), it is in connection with expressions of divine anger against sin. He is also a jealous God (*El Kanna*; EL kan-NAH) who loves us completely and who, therefore, demands our wholehearted response. If we love God, we can be confident of his mercy. Our own zeal will make us jealous for his honor and glory. When you pray these names of God, ask him to give both you and his church a deeper understanding of his holiness and a greater desire to honor and exalt his name.

Be careful not to forget the covenant of the LORD your God that he made with you; do not make for yourselves an idol in the form of anything the LORD your God has forbidden. For the LORD your God is Esh Oklah, El Kanna.
— DEUTERONOMY 4:23–24

Consuming Fire; Jealous God
ESH OKLAH, EL KANNA
∞

Understanding the Name

Read Exodus 34:10–19.

Why do you think the Lord says his name is "Jealous"?

_____

_____

_____

_____

_____

_____

How does this name of God relate to your own life? To the church today?

_____

_____

_____

_____

_____

_____

_____

_____

_____

_____

_____

_____

_____

Tuesday

Consuming Fire; Jealous God

Esh Oklah, El Kanna

Praying the Name

Esh Oklah, you promise to be a wall of fire protecting Jerusalem and to be its glory within. Be a wall of fire around me, and help me to remember that you, *Esh Oklah*, protect me. Then use your consuming fire to burn away my sin and make your glory blaze within me.

(Zechariah 2:5)

Wednesday
Consuming Fire; Jealous God
Esh Oklah, El Kanna

Praying the Name

Esh Oklah, when you came into my life, you were like a refiner's fire, burning away the impurities in me; you were like a launderer's soap that washed me clean. No matter how painful the process, please continue to purify and refine me so that I can stand on the day of your return.

(Malachi 3:2–3)

Thursday

Consuming Fire; Jealous God

ESH OKLAH, EL KANNA

Praying the Name

El Kanna, your love for me is as strong as death and as unyielding as the grave. It burns like a blazing fire, a mighty flame. Not even a river of water can wash it away. I love you and praise you, my great God, my *El Kanna*. (SONG OF SONGS 8:6–7)

Friday

Consuming Fire; Jealous God
ESH OKLAH, EL KANNA
∞

Promises Associated with *Esh Oklah, El Kanna*

Be careful not to forget the covenant of the LORD your God that he made with you; do not make for yourselves an idol in the form of anything the LORD your God has forbidden. For the LORD your God is a consuming fire, a jealous God.
— DEUTERONOMY 4:23–24

> *"Who of us can dwell with the consuming fire?*
> *Who of us can dwell with everlasting burning?"*
> *He who walks righteously and speaks what is right …*
> — ISAIAH 33:14–15

_____
_____
_____
_____
_____
_____
_____
_____
_____
_____
_____
_____
_____
_____
_____

Monday

Holy One of Israel

קָדוֹשׁ יִשְׂרָאֵל
QEDOSH YISRAEL

To understand the title "Holy One of Israel," *Qedosh Yisrael* (Ke-DOSH yis-ra-AIL), we first need to understand that holiness is grounded in God's nature. "Holy One of Israel" emphasizes God's uniqueness, otherness, and mystery, as well as his call to his people to become holy as he is. The Israelites were to be set apart for God, devoted to his service, and committed to honoring his character by reflecting it in all of their relationships. As believers, we are called to reflect the character of Christ, to be holy even as he is holy. When you pray to the Holy One of Israel, you are praying to the God whose holiness encompasses not only his separation from evil, but also his power, knowledge, justice, mercy, goodness, and love.

The LORD said to Moses, "Speak to the entire assembly of Israel and say to them: 'Be holy because I, Qedosh Yisrael, am holy.'" —LEVITICUS 19:1–2

Holy One of Israel
QEDOSH YISRAEL
⚭

Understanding the Name

Read Leviticus 19:1–18.

In Leviticus 19, God links his commandments to his name. Why do you think he keeps reminding the people that he is "the LORD your God"?

_____

_____

_____

_____

_____

_____

_____

If this were the only passage of Scripture you had ever read, what would it lead you to believe about God's character?

_____

_____

_____

_____

_____

_____

_____

_____

_____

Tuesday
Holy One of Israel
QEDOSH YISRAEL

Praying the Name

Qedosh Yisrael, you are the Holy One of Israel. In your presence the angels cover their faces. I bow down before you and beg you to give me a glimpse of your glory.

(ISAIAH 6:1–4)

Wednesday
Holy One of Israel
QEDOSH YISRAEL
⚬

Praying the Name

Qedosh Yisrael, help me to be an obedient child, to not give in to the evil desires I had when I didn't know you. Help me to be holy in all I do because you are holy and I love you and want to please you.

(1 PETER 1:14–16)

Thursday
Holy One of Israel
QEDOSH YISRAEL

Praying the Name

Qedosh Yisrael, you call us to be holy as you are holy. Please give me the strength and the courage to follow you no matter what others are doing. Lord, bless and purify your church.

(1 CORINTHIANS 5:11)

Friday
Holy One of Israel
QEDOSH YISRAEL
∞

Promises Associated with *Qedosh Yisrael*

> *"This is the covenant I will make with the house of Israel*
>   *after that time," declares the LORD.*
> *"I will put my law in their minds*
>   *and write it on their hearts.*
> *I will be their God,*
>   *and they will be my people."*
> —JEREMIAH 31:33

...by one sacrifice he [Christ] has made perfect forever those who are being made holy.

> The Holy Spirit also testifies to us about this. First he says:

> *"This is the covenant I will make with them*
>   *after that time, says the Lord.*
> *I will put my laws in their hearts,*
>   *and I will write them on their minds."*
> —HEBREWS 10:14-16

"For God so loved the world that he gave his one and only Son, that whoever believes in him shall not perish but have eternal life. For God did not send his Son into the world to condemn the world, but to save the world through him."
> —JOHN 3:16-17

_____

_____

_____

_____

_____

_____

_____

Monday

The LORD Is Peace

יְהוָה שָׁלוֹם

YAHWEH SHALOM

⬥

Yahweh Shalom (yah-WEH sha-LOME) is a title rather than a name. *Shalom* is a Hebrew word much richer in its range of meanings than the English word *peace*. The concept of *shalom* includes "wholeness," "completeness," "finished word," "perfection," "safety," or "wellness." *Shalom* is a common term for greeting or saying farewell in modern Israel. In its deepest meaning, it expresses the hope that the person may be well in every sense of the word—fulfilled, satisfied, prosperous, healthy, and in harmony with herself, others, and God. When you pray to *Yahweh Shalom,* you are praying to the source of all peace.

So Gideon built an altar to the LORD there and called it Yahweh Shalom.
—JUDGES 6:24

The LORD Is Peace
YAHWEH SHALOM

Understanding the Name

Read Judges 6:1–24.

Think about a time in your life when you felt harassed by circumstances. What caused your difficulties, and how did you respond to them?

_____

_____

_____

_____

_____

_____

_____

_____

_____

What comes to mind when you hear the word *peace?*

_____

_____

_____

_____

_____

_____

_____

_____

_____

_____

_____

Tuesday
The LORD Is Peace
YAHWEH SHALOM

∞∞∞

Praying the Name

Yahweh Shalom, like Gideon, I realize that I am a sinful person who can't look you in the face. My sin robs me of peace—but you offer me your peace. Like you told Gideon, you tell me not to be afraid. Help me to confess my sins and know you as *Yahweh Shalom*.

(JUDGES 6:22–24)

_____

_____

_____

_____

_____

_____

_____

_____

_____

_____

_____

_____

_____

_____

_____

_____

_____

_____

_____

Wednesday

The LORD Is Peace
YAHWEH SHALOM

Praying the Name

Yahweh Shalom, I am anxious about many things. But you promise in your Word that if I pray about everything, if I give you all my requests and worries, and thank you, you will give me your peace in Christ Jesus, a peace that goes beyond anything I have ever known.

(PHILIPPIANS 4:6–7)

Thursday
The LORD Is Peace
YAHWEH SHALOM

Praying the Name

Yahweh Shalom, Jerusalem seems like the least peaceful place on earth. But for the sake of my brothers and sisters who live there, and for your people who love you, and so that peace may come to the whole world, I pray for the peace of Jerusalem.

(PSALM 122:6–8)

Friday

The LORD Is Peace

YAHWEH SHALOM

∞

Promises Associated with *Yahweh Shalom*

The fruit of the Spirit is love, joy peace, patience, kindness, goodness, faithfulness, gentleness and self-control. Against such things there is no law.

*—*GALATIANS 5:22

> *Blessed is the man who finds wisdom,*
> *the man who gains understanding,*
> *for she is more profitable than silver*
> *and yields better returns than gold....*
> *Long life is in her right hand;*
> *in her left hand are riches and honor.*
> *Her ways are pleasant ways,*
> *and all her paths are peace.*
> *—*PROVERBS 3:13–14, 16–17

You will keep in perfect peace him whose mind is steadfast, because he trusts in you.   ISAIAH 26:3

"For I know the plans I have for you," declares the LORD, *"plans to prosper you and not to harm you, plans to give you hope and a future. Then you will call upon me and come and pray to me, and I will listen to you. You will seek me and find me when you seek me with all your heart. I will be found by you," declares the* LORD.   *—*JEREMIAH 29:11–14

LORD of Hosts

יהוה צְבָאוֹת

YAHWEH TSEBAOTH

∞

Yahweh Tsebaoth (yah-WEH tse-ba-OATH) is a title of great power. It occurs more than 240 times in the Old Testament, reminding us that all of creation, even in its fallen condition, is under God's rule and reign. When Scripture speaks of "the host of heaven," it is usually speaking of celestial bodies, although the phrase can also refer to angelic beings. The word *host* can also refer to human beings and to nature itself. The NIV translates this title as "LORD Almighty." When you pray to *Yahweh Tsebaoth*, you are praying to a God so magnificent that all creation serves his purposes.

David said to the Philistine [Goliath], "You come against me with sword and spear and javelin, but I come against you in the name of the Yahweh Tsebaoth, the God of the armies of Israel, whom you have defied. This day the LORD will hand you over to me." —1 SAMUEL 17:45–46

LORD of Hosts
YAHWEH TSEBAOTH
∞

Understanding the Name

Read 1 Samuel 17:38–47.

Contrast David's attitude toward the battle with Goliath's.

_____

_____

_____

_____

_____

_____

_____

_____

Consider the times in your own life when you felt embattled. How did you deal with your struggles?

_____

_____

_____

_____

_____

_____

_____

_____

_____

Tuesday
LORD of Hosts
YAHWEH TSEBAOTH

Praying the Name

Yahweh Tsebaoth, you opened the eyes of Elisha's servant to see the hosts of heaven all around them. Open my eyes to see the ways that you protect me and my family. Help me to remember that those who are with us are greater than those who are with our enemies, both physical and spiritual. (2 KINGS 6:15–17)

Wednesday
LORD of HOSTS
YAHWEH TSEBAOTH

Praying the Name

Yahweh Tsebaoth, though the nations of the earth are in uproar, one word from you would subdue them. Help me to remember this when I am disturbed by the news today. And thank you for being not only the Lord of Hosts but my God too. (PSALM 46:6–7)

Thursday
LORD of HOSTS
YAHWEH TSEBAOTH
∞

Praying the Name

Yahweh Tsebaoth, your zeal will put the government of the whole world upon the shoulders of your Son, who will bring justice, righteousness, and never-ending peace. I bless you, *Yahweh Tsebaoth*, for making me part of the host of this kingdom of Christ Jesus. (ISAIAH 9:6–7)

_____

_____

_____

_____

_____

_____

_____

_____

_____

_____

_____

_____

_____

_____

_____

_____

_____

_____

_____

_____

Friday
LORD of Hosts
YAHWEH TSEBAOTH
∞

Promises Associated with *Yahweh Tsebaoth*

"Do not be terrified; do not be afraid of them. The LORD your God, who is going before you, will fight for you, as he did for you in Egypt, before your very eyes, and in the desert. There you saw how the LORD your God carried you, as a father carries his son, all the way you went until you reached this place."

—DEUTERONOMY 1:29-31

When you go to war against your enemies and see horses and chariots and an army greater than yours, do not be afraid of them, because the LORD your God, who brought you up out of Egypt, will be with you.

—DEUTERONOMY 20:1

Do not be afraid or terrified because of them, for the LORD your God goes with you; he will never leave you nor forsake you.

—DEUTERONOMY 31:6

Be still, and know that I am God! I am exalted among the nations, I am exalted in the earth. The LORD of hosts is with us, the God of Jacob is our refuge.
—PSALM 46:10-11 (NEW REVISED STANDARD VERSION)

Monday

The LORD My Rock

יהוה צוּרִי

YAHWEH TSURI

What better word than *rock* to represent God's permanence, protection, and enduring faithfulness? Rocks provided shade, shelter, and safety in the wilderness and were used to construct altars, temples, houses, and city walls. God's commandments, given to Moses, were etched on stone so that all generations would learn his law. The Hebrew noun *tsur* is often translated "rock" or "stone." To worship *Yahweh Tsuri* (yah-WEH tsu-REE) is to echo Hannah's great prayer of praise: "There is no Rock like our God" (1 Samuel 2:2). When you pray to the Lord your Rock, you are praying to the God who can always be counted on. His purposes and plans remain firm throughout history.

> *Praise be to Yahweh Tsuri,*
> *who trains my hands for war,*
> *my fingers for battle.*
> —PSALM 144:1

The Lord My Rock
Yahweh Tsuri
∞

Understanding the Name

Read Psalm 144:1–10.

David expressed his sense of vulnerability with vivid images. Describe a time in your life when you felt particularly vulnerable.

_____

_____

_____

_____

_____

_____

_____

_____

How would your life be different If you experienced more deeply the truth that God is your Rock?

_____

_____

_____

_____

_____

_____

_____

_____

Tuesday
The LORD My Rock
YAHWEH TSURI

Praying the Name

Yahweh Tsuri, you are my fortress—I can run to you for protection. You are my deliverer—you rescue me from trouble. You are my shield—you keep me from being wounded by my enemies. You are my refuge—in you I can be secure. (2 SAMUEL 22:2–3)

Wednesday
The LORD My Rock
YAHWEH TSURI

Praying the Name

Yahweh Tsuri, you promise that those who trust in you can never be shaken. I am shaky when I don't trust in you. Help me to remember that you surround me with your strength and your love always and no matter what.

(PSALM 125:1–2)

Thursday
The LORD My Rock
YAHWEH TSURI

Praying the Name

Yahweh Tsuri, help me to study your Word and then do what it says, just like the wise man whom Jesus described as building his house on the rock. Then when trouble, fear, and confusion surround me, I will not collapse because my thinking and living are founded on the rock of your Truth.

(MATTHEW 7:24–25)

Friday
The LORD My Rock
YAHWEH TSURI
∞

Promises Associated with *Yahweh Tsuri*

You will keep in perfect peace
*   him whose mind is steadfast,*
*   because he trusts in you.*
Trust in the LORD forever,
*   for the LORD, the LORD, is the Rock eternal.*
*   —ISAIAH 26:3–4*

My soul finds rest in God alone;
*   my salvation comes from him.*
He alone is my rock and my salvation;
*   he is my fortress, I will never be shaken.*
*   —PSALM 62:1–2*

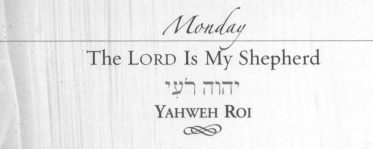

Monday

The LORD Is My Shepherd

יהוה רֹעִי

YAHWEH ROI

The Hebrew Scriptures speak of God as the Shepherd (yah-WEH row-EE) of his people, and they apply this image to religious leaders as well. The New Testament presents Jesus as the Good Shepherd who protects the lives of his sheep by forfeiting his own life. When you pray to the Lord your Shepherd, you are praying to the one who watches over you day and night, feeding you and leading you safely on the path of righteousness.

> *Yahweh Roi, I shall not be in want.*
> *He makes me lie down in green pastures,*
> *he leads me beside quiet waters,*
> *he restores my soul.*
> *He guides me in paths of righteousness*
> *for his name's sake.*
>
> —PSALM 23:1–3

_____

_____

_____

_____

_____

_____

_____

_____

_____

_____

_____

_____

The LORD Is My Shepherd
YAHWEH ROI
⬥

Understanding the Name

Read Psalm 23.

Imagine that you are a sheep. What do you see? What do you feel?

_____

_____

_____

_____

_____

_____

_____

_____

How would your experience of daily life change if you really believed that goodness and kindness would follow you all the days of your life?

_____

_____

_____

_____

_____

_____

_____

_____

_____

Tuesday

The LORD Is My Shepherd

YAHWEH ROI

Praying the Name

Yahweh Roi, I walk through dark and dangerous times, but I don't need to be afraid because you are with me. Help me to lean on your strong arm that wards off my enemies. Help me to feel your gentle staff touching me with the comfort of your presence. (PSALM 23:4)

Wednesday

The LORD Is My Shepherd

YAHWEH ROI

Praying the Name

Yahweh Roi, please help my family members to put Jesus at the center of their lives, to follow him as their shepherd. For I know only Jesus can lead them to springs of living water—to real, meaningful, and purposeful lives. I pray that you will bless them today. (REVELATION 7:17)

Thursday

The LORD Is My Shepherd

YAHWEH ROI

Praying the Name

Yahweh Roi, you tend me and all of your flock like a shepherd. You gather me in your arms and carry me close to your heart, even when I kick my sharp hooves and squirm and bleat. Help me to relax and to feel your gentle and strong arms around me.   (ISAIAH 40:11)

Friday
The LORD Is My Shepherd
YAHWEH ROI
∞

Promises Associated with *Yahweh Roi*

I myself will tend my sheep and have them lie down, declares the Sovereign LORD. I will search for the lost and bring back the strays. I will bind up the injured and strengthen the weak, but the sleek and the strong I will destroy. I will shepherd the flock with justice. —EZEKIEL 34:15-16

"I am the good shepherd; I know my sheep and my sheep know me— just as the Father knows me and I know the Father—and I lay down my life for the sheep. I have other sheep that are not of this sheep pen. I must bring them also. They too will listen to my voice, and there shall be one flock and one shepherd." —JOHN 10:14-18

Monday
The Name
הַשֵּׁם
HASHEM
∽

Shem is the Hebrew word for "name." God's name is associated with his glory, power, holiness, protection, trust, and love. To call on his name is to call on his presence. To act in his name is to act with his authority. To fight in his name is to fight with his power. The Bible speaks of Solomon's temple in Jerusalem as the place where God's name would dwell—the place where his people could pray and be heard. When we pray to *Hashem* (ha-SHAME), we are praying to the holy God who dwells in our midst, hearing and answering our prayers.

"Hear the cry and the prayer that your servant [Solomon] is praying in your presence this day. May your eyes be open toward this temple night and day, this place of which you said, 'Hashem shall be there,' so that you will hear the prayer your servant prays toward this place." —1 KINGS 8:28–29

_____

_____

_____

_____

_____

_____

_____

_____

_____

_____

_____

The Name
HASHEM
∞

Understanding the Name

Read 1 Kings 8:22–9:3.

What does it mean to confess God's name? What is the connection between repentance and answered prayer?

_____

_____

_____

_____

_____

_____

_____

_____

What does God mean when he says he will put his "Name" in the temple?

_____

_____

_____

_____

_____

_____

_____

_____

_____

Tuesday
The Name
HASHEM

Praying the Name

Hahem, as you heard the prayer of Solomon and put your name on the temple, so you have heard my prayer and put your name on me through the power of your Holy Spirit. Help me understand that I am your temple and that your eyes and your heart will always be with me.   (1 KINGS 9:3)

Wednesday
The Name
HASHEM

Praying the Name

Hashem, I praise your name because it is holy. I praise your name because it reveals who you are. I praise your name because it is powerful. When I call upon that name, the King of the Universe answers me—because you have made me yours. (PSALM 30:4)

Thursday
The Name
HASHEM

Praying the Name

Hashem, I live in a dark world, filled with dark thoughts and dark actions. But you promise that you will enable me to walk through this darkness if I trust in your name and rely on you. Please help me not to fear the dark but to trust you to guide me as I follow the light of Jesus.

(ISAIAH 50:10)

Friday
The Name
HASHEM

∞

Promises Associated with *Hashem*

"Because he loves me," says the LORD, *"I will rescue him;*
I will protect him, for he acknowledges my name.
He will call upon me, and I will answer him;
I will be with him in trouble,
I will deliver him and honor him.

—PSALM 91:14–15

Turn to me and have mercy on me,
as you always do to those who love your name.

—PSALM 119:132

The LORD *will establish you as his holy people, as he promised you on oath, if*
you keep the commands of the LORD *your God and walk in his ways. Then all*
the peoples on earth will see that you are called by the name of the LORD, *and*
they will fear you. The LORD *will grant you abundant prosperity—in the fruit*
of your womb, the young of your livestock and the crops of your ground—in the
land he swore to your forefathers to give you. —DEUTERONOMY 28:9–11

Monday

King

יהוה מֶלֶךְ

YAHWEH MELEK

The Israelites believed that *Yahweh* was *Melek,* or King—not just over Israel, but over every nation on earth. They understood that the temple in Jerusalem was the earthly symbol of God's heavenly throne, and they expected a coming Messiah who would one day save his people from their enemies, establishing his rule over the whole world. When you pray to *Yahweh Melek* (yah-WEH ME-lek), you are praying to the God who watches over the whole earth and who will one day come in glory to usher in an eternal kingdom of peace and righteousness.

> *Endow the king with your justice, O God,*
> *the royal son with your righteousness.*
> *He will judge your people in righteousness,*
> *your afflicted ones with justice.*
> *The mountains will bring prosperity to the people,*
> *the hills the fruit of righteousness.*
> —PSALM 72:1–3

King

YAHWEH MELEK

❦

Understanding the Name

Read Psalm 72:1–15.

How would the world be different if today's rulers reflected the values expressed in this psalm?

_____

_____

_____

_____

_____

_____

_____

How have you experienced Jesus' rule in your own life? What difference has it made?

_____

_____

_____

_____

_____

_____

_____

_____

_____

_____

Tuesday
King
YAHWEH MELEK

Praying the Name

Yahweh Melek, I long for the day when you establish your holy kingdom, bring an end to violence and destruction, and fill the earth with the knowledge of you. Help me to know you as *Melek* now and be filled with you like water fills the sea. (ISAIAH 11:9)

Wednesday

King

YAHWEH MELEK

Praying the Name

Yahweh Melek, your kingdom is powerfully advancing as your truth is proclaimed throughout the earth. Help me to take hold of your truth and to have the courage and strength to proclaim your coming kingdom to my generation.

(MATTHEW 11:12)

Thursday
King
YAHWEH MELEK

Praying the Name

Yahweh Melek, you are King of all the earth. You are King of the land and the sky. You are King of all the nations. You raise up rulers and bring them low. Help me to understand your sovereign power, and to trust in your great wisdom as you manage the affairs of the world.

(PSALM 47:7)

Friday
King
YAHWEH MELEK

Promises Associated with *Yahweh Melek*

The LORD will be king over the whole earth. On that day there will be one LORD, and his name the only name. —ZECHARIAH 14:9

"Then the King will say to those on his right, 'Come, you who are blessed by my Father; take your inheritance, the kingdom prepared for you since the creation of the world. For I was hungry and you gave me something to eat, I was thirsty and you gave me something to drink, I was a stranger and you invited me in, I needed clothes and you clothed me, I was sick and you looked after me, I was in prison and you came to visit me.'" —MATTHEW 25:34-36

Then I saw a new heaven and a new earth, for the first heaven and the first earth had passed away, and there was no longer any sea. I saw the Holy City, the new Jerusalem, coming down out of heaven from God, prepared as a bride beautifully dressed for her husband. And I heard a loud voice from the throne saying, "Now the dwelling of God is with men, and he will live with them. They will be his people, and God himself will be with them and be their God. He will wipe every tear from their eyes. There will be no more death or mourning or crying or pain, for the old order of things has passed away." —REVELATION 21:1-4

Monday
Husband

אִישׁ

Ish

❦

God's passionate love for Israel is reflected in the Hebrew word *ish* (EESH), meaning "husband." When it is applied to God in the Hebrew Scriptures, it symbolizes the ideal relationship between God and Israel. God is the perfect husband—loving, forgiving, and faithful, providing for and protecting his people. This metaphor of monogamous marriage between God and his people is strengthened in the New Testament, which reveals Jesus as the loving, sacrificial bridegroom of the church. Our destiny, our greatest purpose as God's people, is to become his bride.

> *"In that day," declares the* LORD,
>> *"you will call me 'my husband';*
>> *you will no longer call me 'my master.'* . . .
> *I will betroth you to me forever;*
>> *I will betroth you in righteousness and justice,*
>> *in love and compassion.*
> *I will betroth you in faithfulness,*
>> *and you will acknowledge the* LORD.*"*
>> —HOSEA 2:16, 19–20

Husband
Ish
∞

Understanding the Name

Read Hosea 1–3.

Put yourself in Hosea's place and imagine how you would feel if your spouse were a prostitute or a womanizer. Now think about how God feels when his people stray from him. What are your thoughts?

_____

_____

_____

_____

_____

_____

_____

What encouragement for your own life can you take from the story of Hosea and Gomer?

_____

_____

_____

_____

_____

_____

_____

_____

_____

Tuesday
Husband
Ish

Praying the Name

Ish, out of all the people in the world, you chose to betroth yourself to me. You chose to give me your love and your compassion. You chose to be faithful to me *forever*, even when I am not faithful to you. Help me to acknowledge you alone as Lord. (HOSEA 2:19–20)

Wednesday
Husband
Ish

Praying the Name

Ish, your Word tells the story of how you love Israel, even though time and time again she played the adulteress by worshiping others. Help me to remember that you love me the same way. Never let me wander from you, and never stop pursuing me with your love.   (HOSEA 3:1)

Thursday
Husband
ISH

Praying the Name

Ish, an idol is anything in my life that takes first place, smothering my love for you. If I've payed homage to idols forgive me and show me what they are. Help me to praise and worship you alone!   (EXODUS 20:4–5)

Friday
Husband
ISH

∽

Promises Associated with *Ish*

"For your Maker is your husband—
    the LORD Almighty is his name—
the Holy One of Israel is your Redeemer;
    he is called the God of all the earth.
The LORD will call you back
    as if you were a wife deserted and distressed in spirit—
a wife who married young,
    only to be rejected," says your God.
"For a brief moment I abandoned you,
    but with deep compassion I will bring you back.
In a surge of anger
    I hid my face from you for a moment,
but with everlasting kindness
    I will have compassion on you,"
    says the LORD your Redeemer.

—ISAIAH 54:5–8

No longer will they call you Deserted,
    or name your land Desolate.
But you will be called Hephzibah [meaning "my delight is in her"],
    and your land Beulah [meaning "married"];
for the Lord will take delight in you
    and your land will be married.
As a young man marries a maiden
    so will your sons marry you;
as a bridegroom rejoices over his bride,
    so will your God rejoice over you.

—ISAIAH 62:4–5

Monday
Living God
אֱלֹהִים חָי
ELOHIM CHAY
∞

The title *Elohim Chay* (e-lo-HEEM CHAY), the Living God, emphasizes God's role as the creator of all that is, in contrast with idols made of metal, wood, or stone, which are merely the creations of human hands. Scripture constantly warns against the worship of false gods. Jeremiah paints a vivid picture, saying, "Like a scarecrow in a melon patch, their idols cannot speak; they must be carried because they cannot walk. Do not fear them; they can do no harm nor can they do any good" (Jeremiah 10:5). Unlike idols of wood and stone, the Living God is himself Maker of heaven and earth. He alone is the source of our life. We live because he lives.

Hezekiah prayed to the LORD: "O LORD, God of Israel, enthroned between the cherubim, you alone are God over all the kingdoms of the earth. You have made heaven and earth. Give ear, O LORD, and hear; open your eyes, O LORD, and see; listen to the words Sennacherib has sent to insult Elohim Chay."

—2 KINGS 19:15–16

Living God

Elohim Chay

∞

Understanding the Name

Read 2 Kings 19:9–37.

How does Hezekiah's prayer reflect his understanding of the "Living God"?

_____

_____

_____

_____

_____

_____

_____

How can this story of Hezekiah's reliance on the Living God be applied in the lives of God's people today? In your own life?

_____

_____

_____

_____

_____

_____

_____

_____

_____

_____

Tuesday
Living God
Elohim Chay

Praying the Name

Elohim Chay, it is true that many people today doubt your existence. They say that God is dead and they set themselves up as gods. Help me to show your truth through my life—the truth that you are *Elohim Chay*, that you alone are God. (2 KINGS 19:15–19)

Wednesday
Living God
ELOHIM CHAY

⸎

Praying the Name

Elohim Chay, I have not heard your voice speaking to me out of fire, like the Israelites did. But I am still in awe of you, the Living God, for I see you working in my life, and I hear you through your Word, through your people, and through your Spirit within me.

(DEUTERONOMY 5:26)

Thursday
Living God
ELOHIM CHAY

Praying the Name

Elohim Chay, my spirit is alive because the Spirit who raised Jesus from the dead is living in me. And although my body is growing old and will someday die, you will give it life again through the same Spirit that lives in me. O *Elohim Chay*, help me to understand what it means to be alive in you.

(ROMANS 8:10–11)

Friday
Living God
ELOHIM CHAY
∞

Promises Associated with *El Chay*

The Samaritan woman said to him, "You are a Jew and I am a Samaritan woman. How can you ask me for a drink?" (For Jews do not associate with Samaritans.)

Jesus answered her, "If you knew the gift of God and who it is that asks you for a drink, you would have asked him and he would have given you living water."

"Sir," the woman said, "you have nothing to draw with and the well is deep. Where can you get this living water? Are you greater than our father Jacob, who gave us the well and drank from it himself, as did also his sons and his flocks and herds?"

Jesus answered, "Everyone who drinks this water will be thirsty again, but whoever drinks the water I give him will never thirst. Indeed, the water I give him will become in him a spring of water welling up to eternal life."

—JOHN 4:9–13

On the last and greatest day of the Feast, Jesus stood and said in a loud voice, "If anyone is thirsty, let him come to me and drink. Whoever believes in me, as the Scripture has said, streams of living water will flow from within him." By this he meant the Spirit, whom those who believed in him were later to receive. Up to that time the Spirit had not been given, since Jesus had not yet been glorified.

—JOHN 7:37–39

Monday

Dwelling Place, Refuge, Shield, Fortress, Strong Tower

מִגְדַּל־עֹז מְצוּדָה מָגֵן מַחְסֶה מָעוֹן

Maon, Machseh, Magen, Metsuda, Migdal-Oz

∞

These descriptive names for God often appear in clusters in the psalms as well as in other portions of Scripture, God is pictured as our Dwelling Place, or *Maon* (ma-OHN), and as our Refuge, or *Machseh* (mach-SEH). A shield, or *Magen* (ma-GAIN), offers another image of God's protecting care. God is also compared to a fortress, or *Metsuda* (me-tsu-DAH), and to a strong tower, or *Migdal-Oz* (mig-dal OHZ). When you pray to God your Refuge, Shield, Fortress, Dwelling Place, and Strong Tower, you are invoking the God who has promised to watch over you and keep you safe.

> *He who dwells in the shelter of the Most High*
> *will rest in the shadow of the Almighty.*
> *I will say of the LORD, "He is my refuge and my fortress,*
> *my God, in whom I trust."*
> —PSALM 91:1–2

_____

_____

_____

_____

_____

_____

_____

_____

_____

_____

Dwelling Place, Refuge, Shield, Fortress, Strong Tower

MAON, MACHSEH, MAGEN, METSUDA, MIGDAL-OZ

∞

Understanding the Name

Read Psalm 91:1–16.

How would your life be different if you were able to take shelter under "the wings of God"?

_____

_____

_____

_____

_____

_____

_____

What dangers does the psalmist list in Psalm 91? What promises from God does he cite?

_____

_____

_____

_____

_____

_____

_____

_____

Tuesday

Dwelling Place, Refuge, Shield, Fortress, Strong Tower

MAON, MACHSEH, MAGEN, METSUDA, MIGDAL-OZ

Praying the Name

Machseh, from you I can find relief when I am oppressed. *Migdal-Oz,* I can run into you for safety in times of trouble. I know your name and I trust in you, for you have shown me that you never forget or leave those who seek you. (PSALM 9:9–10)

Wednesday

Dwelling Place, Refuge, Shield, Fortress, Strong Tower

MAON, MACHSEH, MAGEN, METSUDA, MIGDAL-OZ

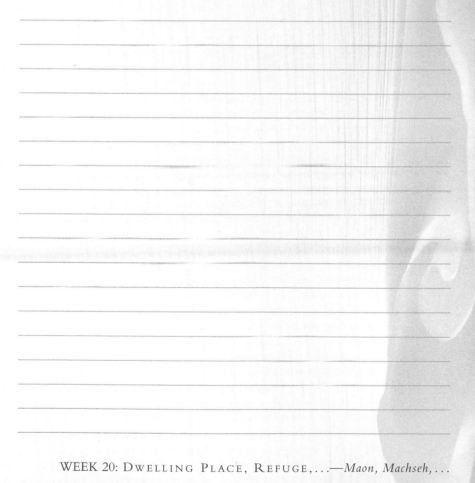

Praying the Name

You, O Lord, have been my *Machseh*, my *Migdal-Oz* against my enemies. Hear my cries and listen to my prayers. I feel like I am calling to you from the ends of the earth and my heart is growing faint with fear. Lead me to you—a rock that is higher than I. (PSALM 61:1–3)

Thursday

Dwelling Place, Refuge, Shield, Fortress, Strong Tower

MAON, MACHSEH, MAGEN, METSUDA, MIGDAL-OZ

Praying the Name

People around me say that I am foolish to follow you and trust you to help and protect me. But you are *Magen* around me, O Lord. And that shield reflects your glory upon me and makes me able to lift up my head in the middle of my trouble. (PSALM 3:2–3)

Friday

Dwelling Place, Refuge, Shield, Fortress, Strong Tower

MAON, MACHSEH, MAGEN, METSUDA, MIGDAL-OZ

∞

Promises Associated with *Maon, Machseh, Magen, Metsuda, Migdal-Oz*

> For surely, O LORD, you bless the righteous;
>   you surround them with your favor as with a shield.
> > —PSALM 5:12

> The name of the LORD is a strong tower;
>   the righteous run to it and are safe.
> > —PROVERBS 18:10

> When calamity comes, the wicked are brought down,
>   but even in death the righteous have a refuge.
> > —PROVERBS 14:32

Monday

Judge

שֹׁפֵט

SHOPHET

Justice is ultimately rooted not in a collection of laws or rules, but in the very character and nature of God. As Judge of the whole earth, he is the only one competent to measure the motives of our hearts. In the Hebrew Scriptures, the word *judge* is often parallel to the word *king*. When we pray to God our *Shophet* (sho-PHAIT), we are praying to the one whose righteousness demands perfect justice, but who has also provided a way for us to be acquitted of our guilt through the life, death, and resurrection of his Son.

> *Judgment will again be founded on righteousness,*
> *and all the upright in heart will follow it.*
> —PSALM 94:15

Judge
SHOPHET
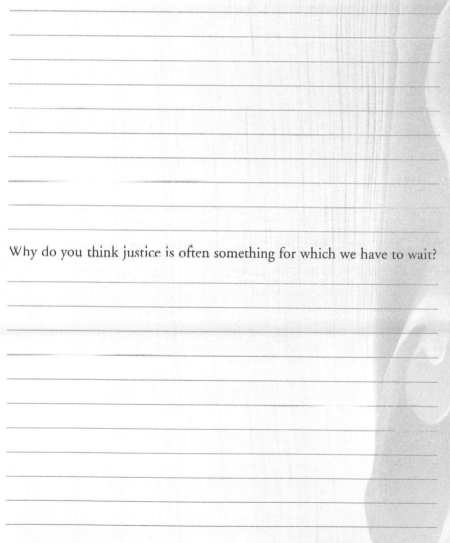

Understanding the Name

Read Psalm 94:2–15.

What reason does the psalmist give for the brazenness of those who do evil? How does this perception of God shape our own world?

_____

_____

_____

_____

_____

_____

_____

_____

Why do you think justice is often something for which we have to wait?

_____

_____

_____

_____

_____

_____

_____

_____

_____

Tuesday

Judge

SHOPHET

Praying the Name

Shophet, you are the only one perfect enough to qualify as Judge for the people of the earth. I am *not* qualified. Please help me to remember this when I am tempted to judge others and to remember that I will be judged by the same scale I myself use in judgment. (MATTHEW 7:1–2)

Wednesday
Judge
SHOPHET

Praying the Name

Shophet, the world is full of injustice. But all nature will rejoice when you return to judge the earth, because you will judge with righteousness and truth. I look forward to that day and will rejoice with all the earth.

(PSALM 96:12–13)

Thursday
Judge
SHOPHET

Praying the Name

Shophet, one day everyone who has ever lived will be judged before your throne. Give me a heart today for those around me who risk facing your righteous judgment alone—because they do not know your Son.

(REVELATION 20:11–12)

Friday
Judge
SHOPHET

Promises Associated with *Shophet*

> *Yet the LORD longs to be gracious to you;*
> *he rises to show you compassion.*
> *For the LORD is a God of justice.*
> *Blessed are all who wait for him!*
>
> —ISAIAH 30:18

I tell you the truth, whoever hears my word and believes him who sent me has eternal life and will not be condemned; he has crossed over from death to life. I tell you the truth, a time is coming and has now come when the dead will hear the voice of the Son of God and those who hear will live. For as the Father has life in himself, so he has granted the Son to have life in himself. And he has given him authority to judge because he is the Son of Man. —JOHN 5:24–27

"Then the King will say to those on his right, 'Come, you who are blessed by my Father; take your inheritance, the kingdom prepared for you since the creation of the world. For I was hungry and you gave me something to eat, I was thirsty and you gave me something to drink, I was a stranger and you invited me in, I needed clothes and you clothed me, I was sick and you looked after me, I was in prison and you came to visit me.'" —MATTHEW 25:34–36

Monday

Hope of Israel

מִקְוֵה יִשְׂרָאֵל
MIQWEH YISRAEL

In the Hebrew Scriptures, hope is often connected to the expectation that God is a deliverer who will save those who trust in him. The Scriptures urge us to wait confidently for him to act. Hope is what helps us stay on course regardless of circumstances. Biblical hope finds its roots in God and in his goodness, mercy, and power. Though we hope for earthly blessings, our greatest hope is aimed at the life to come, when God will not only wipe away our tears but invite us to share his joy forever. When you pray to *Miqweh Yisrael* (MIK-veh yis-ra-AIL), the Hope of Israel, you are praying to the one who saves all those who trust in him.

> *This is what the LORD says:*
>
> *"Blessed is the man who trusts in the LORD,*
> *whose confidence is in him.*
> *He will be like a tree planted by the water*
> *that sends out its roots by the stream.*
> *It does not fear when heat comes;*
> *its leaves are always green.*
> *It has no worries in a year of drought*
> *and never fails to bear fruit." . . .*
> *O LORD, Miqweh Yisrael,*
> *all who forsake you will be put to shame.*
> *—JEREMIAH 17:7–8, 13*

Hope of Israel
Miqweh Yisrael
⬡

Understanding the Name

Read Jeremiah 17:5–13.

What does it mean to put your trust in other people? Give some examples.

_____

_____

_____

_____

_____

_____

_____

_____

_____

What does it mean to put your hope in the Lord? How have you been able to hope in him?

_____

_____

_____

_____

_____

_____

_____

_____

_____

_____

_____

Tuesday
Hope of Israel
MIQWEH YISRAEL
〰️

Praying the Name

Miqweh Yisrael, when I put my trust you, I can have confidence about the future. Hoping in you is like living next to a stream in the desert—you provide a plentiful supply of living water so I don't need to fear heat or drought. Instead, I can flourish. (JEREMIAH 17:7–8)

Wednesday
Hope of Israel
MIQWEH YISRAEL

Praying the Name

Miqweh Yisrael, you are a God who keeps his promises, and this aspect of your character gives me hope. Help me to make this hope an anchor for my soul, firm and secure—no matter what happens to me, no matter what I see that makes me afraid, come what may.　(HEBREWS 6:17–19)

Thursday

Hope of Israel

MIQWEH YISRAEL

Praying the Name

Miqweh Yisrael, my soul waits for you in hope, even more than the night security guard waits for the morning light. I have put my hope in you because your love for me never fails and because you have redeemed me. Help me never to doubt these truths. (PSALM 130:6–7)

Friday

Hope of Israel
Miqweh Yisrael
∽

Promises Associated with *Miqweh Yisrael*

But the eyes of the LORD are on those who fear him,
on those whose hope is in his unfailing love.
—Psalm 33:18

But those who hope in the LORD
will renew their strength.
—Isaiah 40:31

I tell you the truth, you will weep and mourn while the world rejoices. You will grieve, but your grief will turn to joy. A woman giving birth to a child has pain because her time has come; but when her baby is born she forgets the anguish because of her joy that a child is born into the world. So with you: Now is your time of grief, but I will see you again and you will rejoice, and no one will take away your joy. *—John 16:20-22*

Therefore my heart is glad and my tongue rejoices;
my body also will live in hope,
because you will not abandon me to the grave,
nor will you let your Holy One see decay.
You have made known to me the paths of life;
you will fill me with joy in your presence.
—Acts 2:26-28

_____

_____

_____

_____

_____

_____

_____

Monday
The LORD Our Righteousness
יהוה צִדְקֵנוּ
YAHWEH TSIDQENU
⧂⧂⧂

The Hebrew word *tsedeq* is usually translated as "righteousness," but it can also be translated as "righteous," "honest," "right," "justice," "accurate," "just," "truth," or "integrity." Righteousness primarily involves being in right standing with God. As such it concerns fulfilling the demands of relationship with both God and with others. The prophet Jeremiah predicted the coming of a King who would be called "The LORD Our Righteousness," *Yahweh Tsidqenu* (yah-WEH tsid-KAY-nu). Jesus fulfilled this prophecy by restoring our relationship with God through his life, death, and resurrection. When we pray to The LORD Our Righteousness, we are praying to the one who has intervened on our behalf to restore us to his likeness and therefore to fellowship with himself.

> *In his days Judah will be saved*
> *and Israel will live in safety.*
> *This is the name by which he will be called:*
> *Yahweh Tsidqenu.*
> —JEREMIAH 23:6

_____

_____

_____

_____

_____

_____

_____

_____

_____

_____

The LORD Our Righteousness
YAHWEH TSIDQENU

Understanding the Name

Read Jeremiah 23:5–6, Jeremiah 31:33, and Romans 3:21–24.

Jeremiah reveals that the coming King will be known as "The LORD Our Righteousness." What comes to mind when you hear the word *righteous* or *righteousness*?

_____

_____

_____

_____

_____

_____

_____

_____

How has Jesus' sacrifice affected your relationship with God?

_____

_____

_____

_____

_____

_____

_____

_____

Tuesday
The Lord Our Righteousness
Yahweh Tsidqenu

Praying the Name

Yahweh Tsidqenu, Jesus promised that those who hunger and thirst for righteousness will be filled. Please help me to know good, to do good, and to be good, so that I may reflect your goodness. (Matthew 5:6)

Wednesday
The LORD Our Righteousness
YAHWEH TSIDQENU

Praying the Name

Yahweh Tsidqenu, you came to earth so that I could become righteous. You bore my sins on your body on the cross so that the evil in me could be killed and goodness come alive. By your wounds, I am healed. Because of you, I can be truly good. (1 PETER 2:24)

Thursday
The LORD Our Righteousness
YAHWEH TSIDQENU

Praying the Name

Yahweh Tsidqenu, I thought that I knew what righteousness was and that I was a pretty good person. But now that I have seen you in your Word and in my life, I realize that I am not even close to your goodness. Help me to repent of all my sins and to be righteous because you are righteous.

(JOB 42:5–6)

Friday

The LORD Our Righteousness

YAHWEH TSIDQENU

∽

Promises Associated with *Yahweh Tsidqenu*

Blessings crown the head of the righteous.
—PROVERBS 10:6

The memory of the righteous will be a blessing.
—PROVERBS 10:7

The man of integrity walks securely.
—PROVERBS 10:9

The mouth of the righteous is a fountain of life.
—PROVERBS 10:11

The lips of the righteous nourish many.
—PROVERBS 10:21

What the wicked dreads will overtake him;
what the righteous desire will be granted.

When the storm has swept by, the wicked are gone,
but the righteous stand firm forever.
—PROVERBS 10:24–25

The righteous man is rescued from trouble.
—PROVERBS 11:8

Prosperity is the reward of the righteous.
—PROVERBS 13:21

Monday

God Most High

אֵל עֶלְיוֹן

EL ELYON

∞

When applied to God, the term *Elyon*, meaning "Highest" or "Exalted One," emphasizes that God is the highest in every realm of life. The name *El Elyon* (EL el-YOHN) is first used in relation to Melchizedek, the king of Salem, who was also called "priest of God Most High" and who blessed Abraham in the name of "God Most High" (Genesis 14:18–20). In the New Testament, Jesus is known as the Son of the Most High, while the Holy Spirit is the power of the Most High. When you praise the Most High, you are worshiping the one whose power, mercy, and sovereignty cannot be matched.

> *"I praised El Elyon; I honored and glorified him who lives forever.*
> *His dominion is an eternal dominion;*
> *his kingdom endures from generation to generation."*
>
> —DANIEL 4:34

God Most High
EL ELYON
∞

Understanding the Name

Read Daniel 4:19–34.

What do the king's dream and Daniel's interpretation indicate about the source of Nebuchadnezzar's greatness and prosperity?

_____

_____

_____

_____

_____

_____

_____

_____

What can you do to acknowledge God's greatness?

_____

_____

_____

_____

_____

_____

_____

_____

_____

_____

Tuesday
God Most High
EL ELYON

Praying the Name

El Elyon, there is nothing higher than you in all the earth or in the heavens above. You are exalted far above anything or anyone. Help me to remember your position in the universe and to worship only you, *El Elyon*.

(PSALM 97:9)

Wednesday
God Most High
EL ELYON

Praying the Name

El Elyon, Jesus promised that if I love my enemies, do good to them, and lend to them without expecting anything in return, I will have a great reward—and show myself to be a child of *El Elyon*. Help me to be merciful, as you are merciful, so that my life brings glory to you.

(LUKE 6:35–36)

Thursday
God Most High
EL ELYON

Praying the Name

El Elyon, help me to live looking up. Help me to set my heart on things above, where Christ is Most High, instead of on lower, earthly things. Help me to make Jesus my life so that when he appears, I will also appear with him in glory.   (COLOSSIANS 3:1–4)

Friday
God Most High
EL ELYON
⦚

Promises Associated with *El Elyon*

I cry out to God Most High,
to God, who fulfills his purpose for me.
—PSALM 57:2

He who dwells in the shelter of the Most High
will rest in the shadow of the Almighty.
I will say of the LORD, "He is my refuge and my fortress,
my God, in whom I trust."

Surely he will save you from the fowler's snare
and from the deadly pestilence.
He will cover you with his feathers,
and under his wings you will find refuge;
his faithfulness will be your shield and rampart. ...
If you make the Most High your dwelling—
even the LORD, who is my refuge—
then no harm will befall you,
no disaster will come near your tent.
—PSALM 91:1-4, 9-10

Monday

The LORD Is There

יְהוָה שָׁמָּה

YAHWEH SHAMMAH

∞

Strictly speaking, *Yahweh Shammah* is a name for a city rather than a title of God. But it is so closely associated with God's presence and power that it has often been equated with a name for God, at least in popular parlance. The name in the New Testament that is most closely associated with it is *Immanuel,* "God with us," a name that was given to Jesus. *Yahweh Shammah* (yah-WEH SHAM-mah), "The LORD Is There," reminds us that we were created both to enjoy and to manifest God's presence.

This is what the Sovereign LORD says: "The name of the city from that time on will be:

> *Yahweh Shammah."*   —EZEKIEL 48:35

The LORD Is There
YAHWEH SHAMMAH

Understanding the Name

Read Ezekiel 37:21–28; 48:35.

What are the marks of God's presence?

_____

_____

_____

_____

_____

_____

_____

_____

_____

How do you experience God's presence in your life?

_____

_____

_____

_____

_____

_____

_____

_____

_____

_____

Tuesday

The LORD Is There

YAHWEH SHAMMAH

Praying the Name

Yahweh Shammah, you promise to always protect me. When I pass through the waters, you will not let me drown. When I walk through the fire, I will not be burned. You promise to be with me no matter what my trouble.

(ISAIAH 43:2)

Wednesday
The Lord Is There
Yahweh Shammah

Praying the Name

Yahweh Shammah, many times I feel like I am living in the dark. But even the darkness is not dark to you. To you the night shines like day, and because it does, you always know where I am—especially when I am in the dark. (Psalm 139:12)

Thursday
The LORD Is There
YAHWEH SHAMMAH

Praying the Name

Yahweh Shammah, as you are with me, help me also to be with those who are in need—the hungry, the thirsty, the strangers, those who need clothing, the sick, and those in prison. Help me not to focus on myself but to focus on others because that's the path to true blessing.

(MATTHEW 25:41–43)

Friday

The LORD Is There

YAHWEH SHAMMAH

Promises Associated with *Yahweh Shammah*

The virgin will be with child and will give birth to a son, and they will call him Immanuel—which means, "God with us." —MATTHEW 1:23

Consequently, you are no longer foreigners and aliens, but fellow citizens with God's people and members of God's household, built on the foundation of the apostles and prophets, with Christ Jesus himself as the chief cornerstone. In him the whole building is joined together and rises to become a holy temple in the Lord. And in him you too are being built together to become a dwelling in which God lives by his Spirit. —EPHESIANS 2:19-22

Then I saw a new heaven and a new earth, for the first heaven and the first earth had passed away, and there was no longer any sea. I saw the Holy City, the new Jerusalem, coming down out of heaven from God, prepared as a bride beautifully dressed for her husband. And I heard a loud voice from the throne saying, "Now the dwelling of God is with men, and he will live with them. They will be his people, and God himself will be with them and be their God. He will wipe every tear from their eyes. There will be no more death or mourning or crying or pain, for the old order of things has passed away." —REVELATION 21:1-4

Monday
Father
אָב αββα πατήρ
AB, ABBA, PATER

∞

The Hebrew Scriptures normally depict God not as the Father of individuals but as Father to his people, Israel. Pious Jews, aware of the gap between a holy God and sinful human beings, would never have dared address God as *Ab* (Hebrew) or *Abba* (AB-ba), the Aramaic word for "Daddy," which gradually came to mean "dear father." The most frequent term for "father" in the New Testament was the Greek word *pater* (pa-TAIR). Jesus shocked many of his contemporaries by referring to God as his Father and by inviting his followers to call God "Father." Furthermore, by inviting his followers to call God "Father," he made this the primary name by which God is to be known to his followers. That's why we can boldly pray the prayer Jesus taught his disciples: "Our Father in heaven, hallowed be your name."

Jesus said, "While he was still a long way off, his father saw him and was filled with compassion for him; he ran to his son, threw his arms around him and kissed him." —LUKE 15:20

_____

_____

_____

_____

_____

_____

_____

_____

_____

_____

Father

AB, ABBA, PATER

∞

Understanding the Name

Read Luke 15:1–32.

How have you experienced the kind of grace this father extended to his son?

_____

_____

_____

_____

_____

_____

_____

_____

What does this parable reveal about our heavenly Father?

_____

_____

_____

_____

_____

_____

_____

_____

_____

Tuesday
Father
AB, ABBA, PATER

Praying the Name

Pater, like the prodigal son in Jesus' story, you saw me while I was still a long way from you, and you were filled with compassion. You ran to me, dirty as I was, threw your arms around me, and kissed me. Help me to understand your father's love for me. (LUKE 15:20)

Wednesday
Father
AB, ABBA, PATER

Praying the Name

Pater, Jesus said that you are greater than all and that no one can ever snatch me out of your hand. When I am afraid of dangers around me or that you will reject me because of my sin, please help me to remember that I am safe in your hand forever. (JOHN 10:28–30)

Thursday

Father

AB, ABBA, PATER

～～

Praying the Name

*A father to the fatherless, a defender of widows,
    is God in his holy dwelling.
God sets the lonely in families,
    he leads forth the prisoners with singing.*
                                    —PSALM 68:5-6

*As a father has compassion on his children,
    so the LORD has compassion on those who fear him;
for he knows how we are formed,
    he remembers that we are dust.*
                        —PSALM 103:13-14

"See how the lilies of the field grow. They do not labor or spin. Yet I tell you that not even Solomon in all his splendor was dressed like one of these. If that is how God clothes the grass of the field, which is here today and tomorrow is thrown into the fire, will he not much more clothe you, O you of little faith? So do not worry, saying, 'What shall we eat?' or 'What shall we drink?' or 'What shall we wear?' For the pagans run after all these things, and your heavenly Father knows that you need them."   —MATTHEW 6:28-32

"Do not be afraid, little flock, for your Father has been pleased to give you the kingdom."   — LUKE 12:32

I will be a Father to you, and you will be my sons and daughters, says the Lord Almighty.   —2 CORINTHIANS 6:18

Friday
Father
AB, ABBA, PATER

Promises Associated with *Ab, Abba, Pater*

"Whoever has my commands and obeys them, he is the one who loves me. He who loves me will be loved by my Father, and I too will love him and show myself to him." —JOHN 14:21

You did not receive a spirit that makes you a slave again to fear, but you received the Spirit of sonship. And by him we cry, "Abba, Father." The Spirit himself testifies with our spirit that we are God's children. Now if we are children, then we are heirs—heirs of God and co-heirs with Christ, if indeed we share in his sufferings in order that we may also share in his glory. —ROMANS 8:15–17

At Inspirio we love to hear from you—
your stories, your feedback,
and your product ideas.
Please send your comments to us
by way of e-mail at
icares@zondervan.com
or to the address below:

inspirio™

Attn: Inspirio Cares
5300 Patterson Avenue SE
Grand Rapids, MI 49530

If you would like further information
about Inspirio and the products we create,
please visit us at:
www.inspiriogifts.com

Thank you and God bless!